COUNTRY SONGS FOR UKULELE

Strum, Sing, and Pick Along with 30 Cou...

ISBN 978-1-4234-6760-1

HAL•LEONARD®
CORPORATION
7777 W. BLUEMOUND RD. P.O. BOX 13819 MILWAUKEE, WI 53213

Visit Hal Leonard Online at
www.halleonard.com

Achy Breaky Heart
(Don't Tell My Heart)

Words and Music by Don Von Tress

You can tell my feet to hit the floor. Or
self al - read - y knows I'm not o - kay. Or

you can tell my lips to tell my fin - ger - tips they
you can tell my eyes to watch out for my mind. It

won't be reach - ing out for you no more. ___
might be walk - ing out on me to - day. ___   1., 2. But

𝄋 Chorus

don't tell my heart, } my ach - y break - y heart. ___   I
3. Don't tell my heart, }

just don't think he'd un - der - stand.   And

if you tell my heart, my ach - y break - y heart, ___ he

Always on My Mind

Words and Music by Wayne Thompson, Mark James and Johnny Christopher

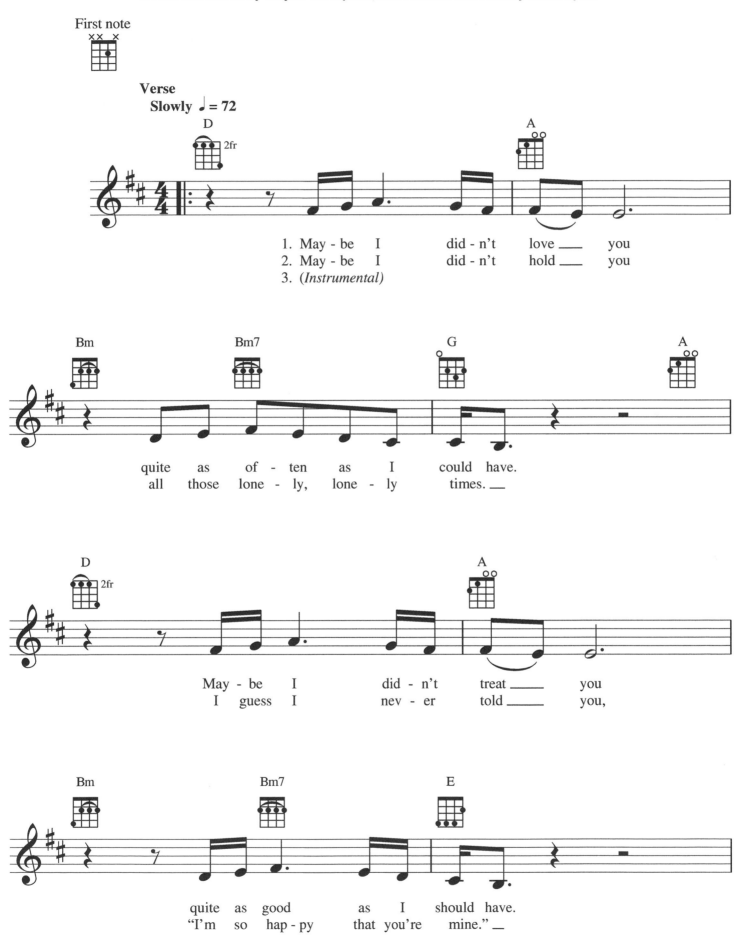

1. May - be I did - n't love ____ you
2. May - be I did - n't hold ____ you
3. *(Instrumental)*

quite as of - ten as I could have.
all those lone - ly, lone - ly times. ____

May - be I did - n't treat ____ you
I guess I nev - er told ____ you,

quite as good as I should have.
"I'm so hap - py that you're mine." ____

(1.) If I made you feel ____ sec-ond best, ____
(2., 3.) Lit-tle things I should have said and done, ____

girl, I'm sor-ry ____ I was blind. ____
I just nev-er ____ took the time. ____

You were al-ways on my ____ mind.

To Coda ⊕

You were al-ways on my ____ mind.

Bridge

Tell ____ me, ____

tell me that your sweet love has-n't died. ____

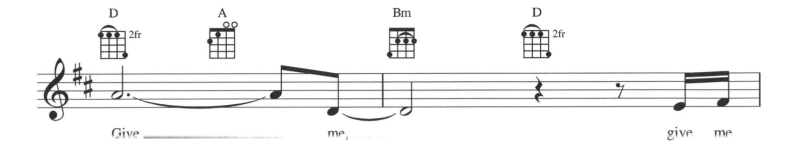

Give _____ me, _____ give me

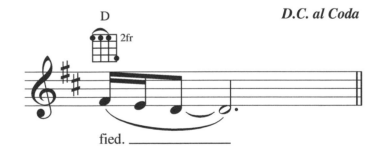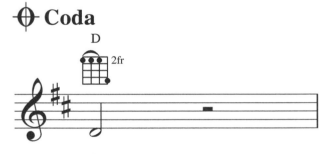

one more chance to keep ___ you sat - is - fied. ____ I'll keep you sat - is -

D.C. al Coda   ⊕ **Coda**

fied. _____   mind.

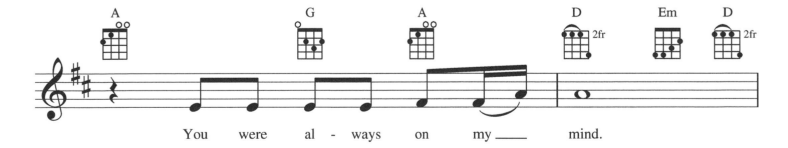

You were al - ways on my ___ mind.

You were al - ways on my ___ mind.

Blue Bayou

Words and Music by Roy Orbison and Joe Melson

First note

Verse
Moderately ♩ = 116

1. I feel so bad, __ I've got a wor - ried mind.

I'm so lone - some all the time since I left my

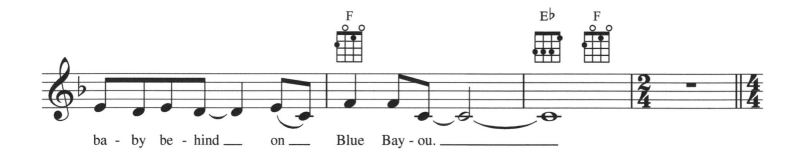

ba - by be - hind __ on __ Blue Bay - ou. _____

Verse

2. Sav - ing nick - els, sav - ing dimes, work - ing 'til the
3. Oh, to see my ba - by a - gain and to be with

sun don't shine, ___ look - ing for - ward to hap - pi - er times ___ on
some of my friends, may - be I'd be hap - py then ___ on

Chorus

F   E♭   F   F

Blue Bay - ou! ___ 1. I'm go - ing back some day, ___
Blue Bay - ou. ___ 2. I'm go - ing back some day, ___

C7

come what may ___ to Blue Bay - ou! _____ Where you
gon - na stay ___ on Blue Bay - ou! _____ Where the

F

sleep all day ___ and the cat - fish play ___ on Blue Bay - ou. _____
folks are fine ___ and the world is mine ___ on Blue Bay - ou. _____

F+

_____ All those fish - ing boats __ with their sails a - float ___ if
_____ Ah, that girl of mine __ by my side, ___ the

I could on - ly see that fa - mil - iar sun - rise _____ through
sil - ver moon and the eve - ning tide, oh, ___ some sweet _ day, _____ gon - na

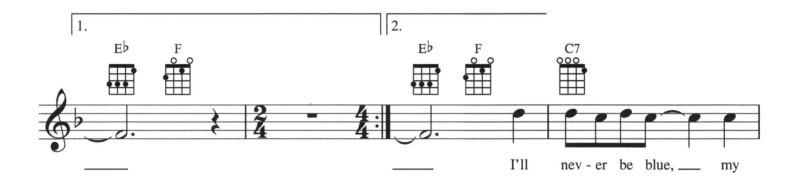

sleep - y eyes, _____ how hap - py I'd be. _____
take a - way _____ this hurt - in' in - side. _____

_____ _____ I'll nev - er be blue, ___ my

dreams _ come true _____ on Blue

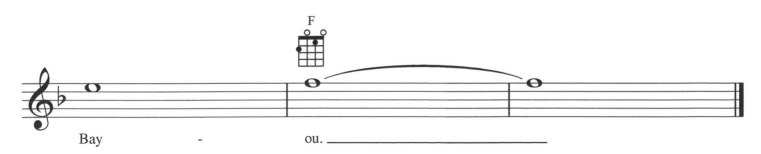

Bay - ou. _____

Chattanoogie Shoe Shine Boy

Words and Music by Harry Stone and Jack Stapp

1. Have you ev- er passed the cor- ner of Fourth and Grand __ where a
(2.) charg- es you a nick- el just to shine one shoe. __ He

lit- tle ball of rhy- thm has a shoe shine stand? __ You
makes the old- est kind of leath- er look like new. __ You

Peo- ple gath- er 'round and they clap __ their hands. __ } He's a
feel as though you want to dance when he gets through. __ }

great, big bun- dle of joy. __ He pops a

boo- gie woo- gie rag, the Chat- ta- noo- gie shoe shine boy. __

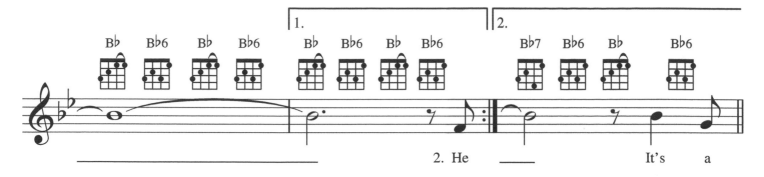

2. He _____ It's a

Bridge

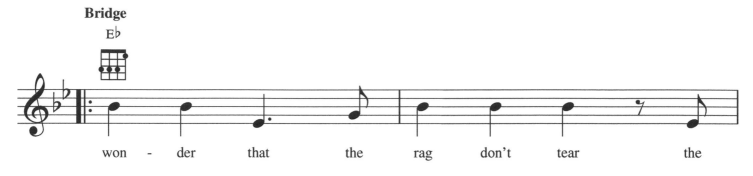

won - der that the rag don't tear the

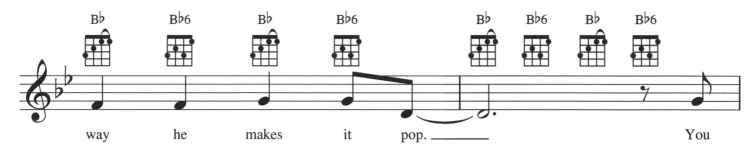

way he makes it pop. _____ You

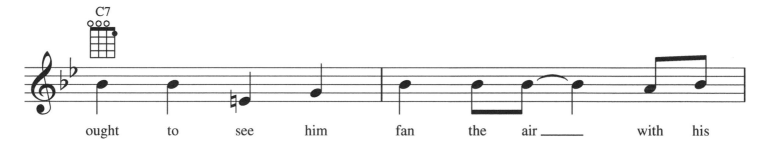

ought to see him fan the air _____ with his

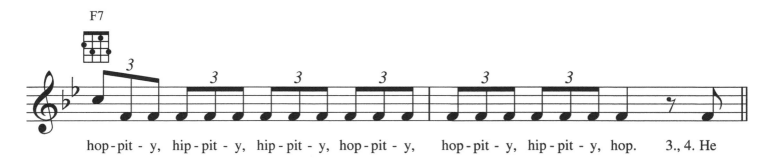

hop-pit-y, hip-pit-y, hip-pit-y, hop-pit-y, hop-pit-y, hip-pit-y, hop. 3., 4. He

Verse

o - pens up for bus'- ness when the clock strikes 9. _____ He

Could I Have This Dance

from URBAN COWBOY

Words and Music by Wayland Holyfield and Bob House

life? Would you be _____ my part - ner _____ ev' - ry

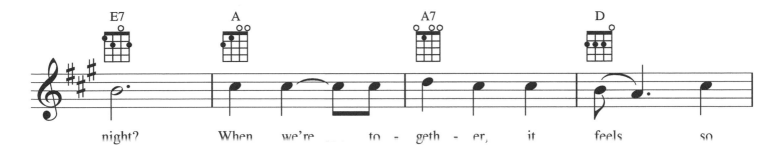

night? When we're _____ to - geth - er, it feels so

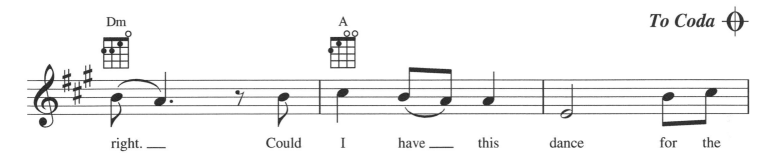

To Coda ⊕

right. ___ Could I have ___ this dance for the

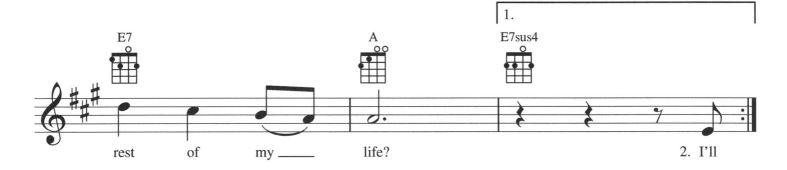

1.

rest of my _____ life? 2. I'll

2.   *D.S. al Coda*   ⊕ **Coda**

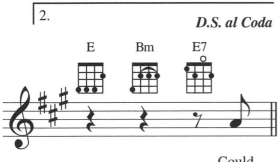

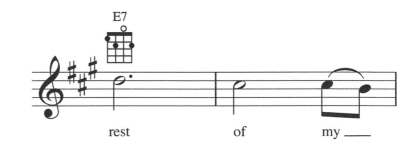

Could   rest of my ___

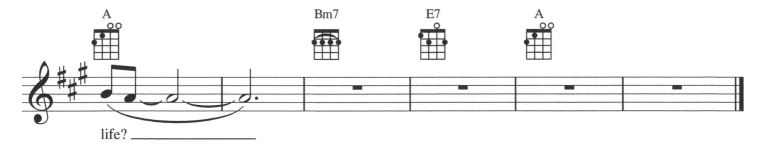

life? _____

Crazy

Words and Music by Willie Nelson

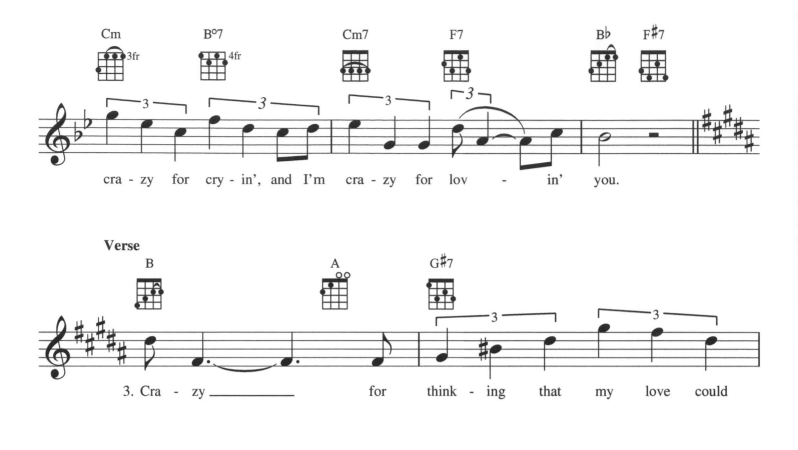

cra - zy for cry - in', and I'm cra - zy for lov - in' you.

Verse

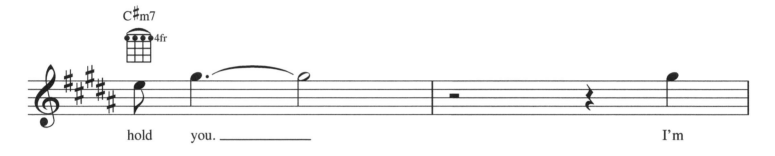

3. Cra - zy _____ for think - ing that my love could

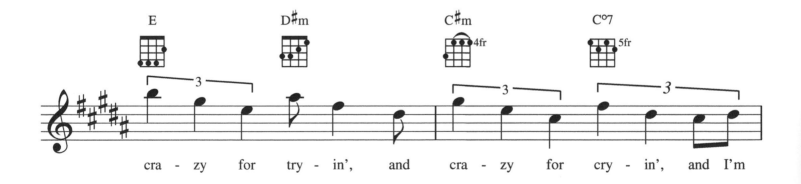

hold you. _____ I'm

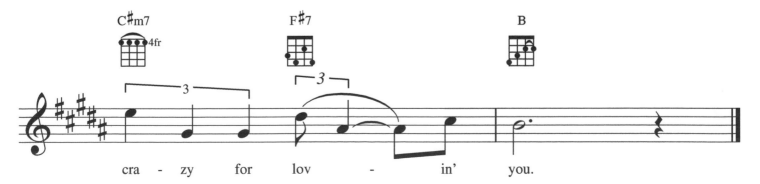

cra - zy for try - in', and cra - zy for cry - in', and I'm

cra - zy for lov - in' you.

Crying in the Chapel

Words and Music by Artie Glenn

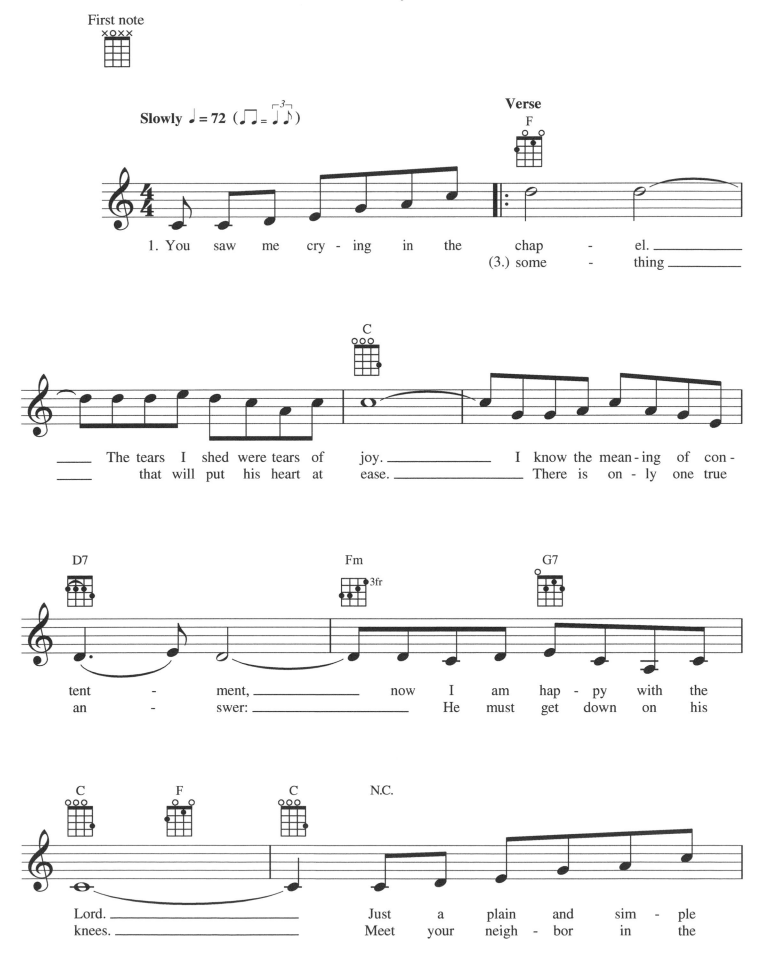

For the Good Times

Words and Music by Kris Kristofferson

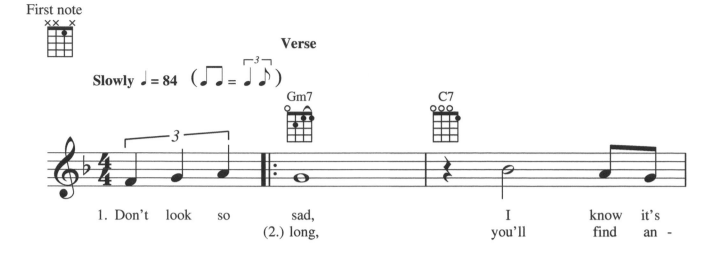

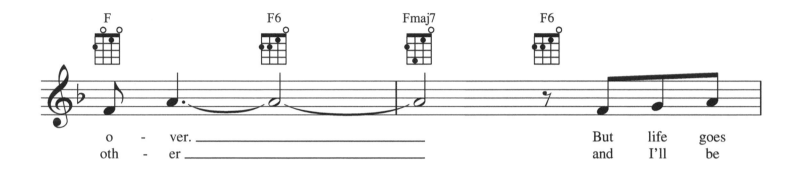

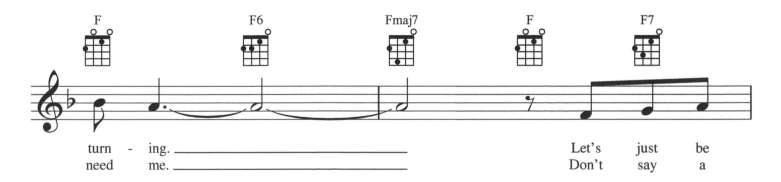

mine. _____ Hear the whis - per of the

rain - drops blow - ing soft a - gainst the win - dow

and make be - lieve you love me _____ one more

time. For the

1.

good times. _____ 2. I'll get a -

2.

good times. _____

The Gambler

Words and Music by Don Schlitz

He said, "Son, I've made a life _____ out of

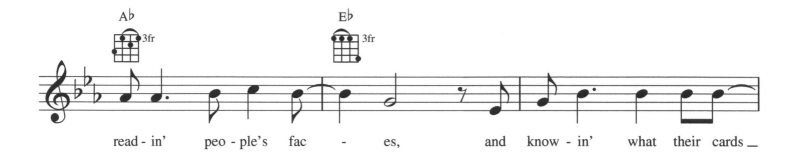

read - in' peo - ple's fac - es, and know - in' what their cards _____

_____ were by the way they held _____ their eyes. _____ And if

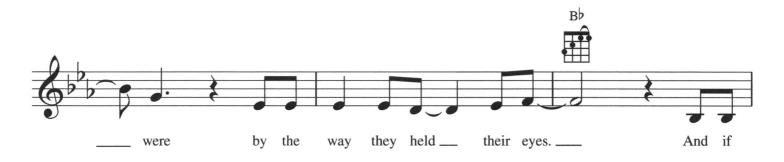

you don't mind _____ my say - in', I can see you're out _____ of a -

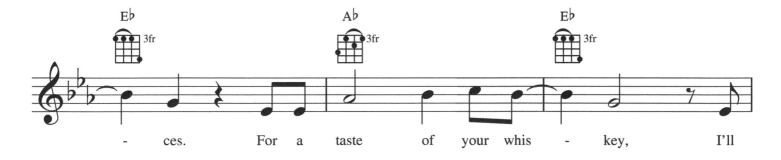

- ces. For a taste of your whis - key, I'll

give you some ad - vice." _____ So I

hand - ed him my bot - tle, and he drank down my last

swal - low. Then he bummed a cig - a - rette ___ and

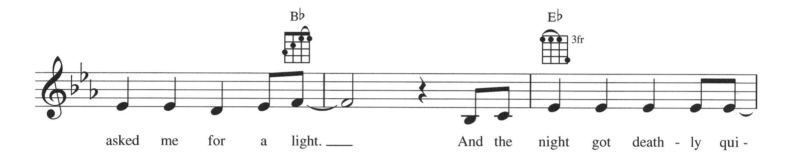

asked me for a light. ___ And the night got death - ly qui -

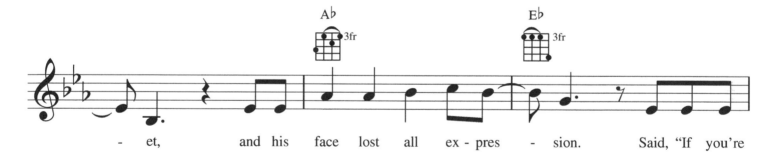

- et, and his face lost all ex - pres - sion. Said, "If you're

gon - na play ___ the game, ___ boy, ya got - ta learn to play ___ it right. ___

Chorus

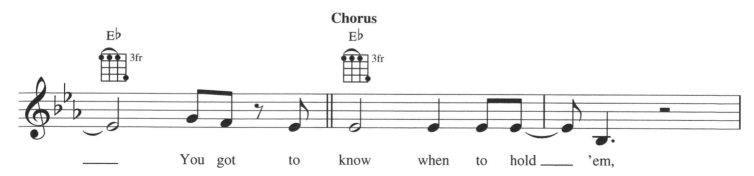

___ You got to know when to hold ___ 'em,

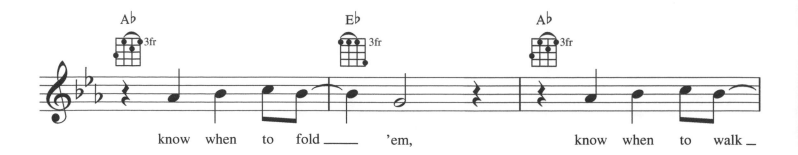

know when to fold _____ 'em,   know when to walk _

_____ a - way, _   and know when to run. _____ You nev - er

count   your   mon - ey   when you're sit - tin'   at   the ta -

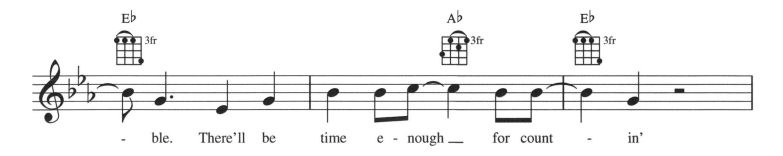

- ble.   There'll be   time   e - nough _ for count - in'

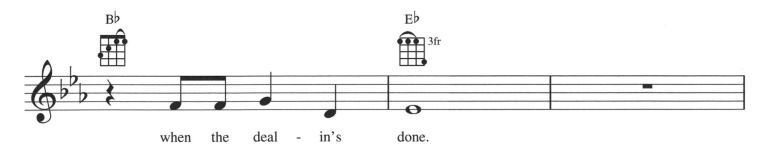

when   the   deal - in's   done.

Verse

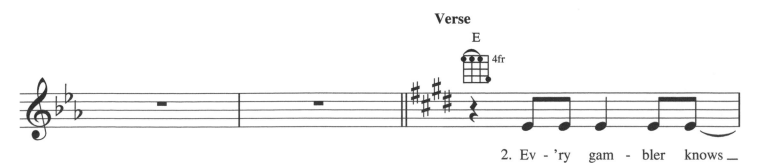

2. Ev - 'ry gam - bler knows _

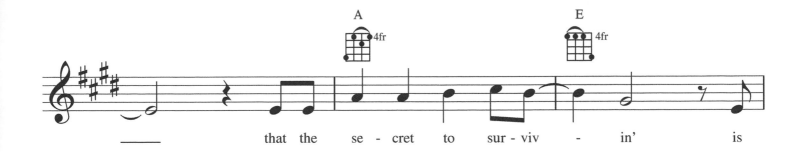

that the se - cret to sur - viv - in' is

know - in' what to throw a - way ___ and know - in' what to keep. ___

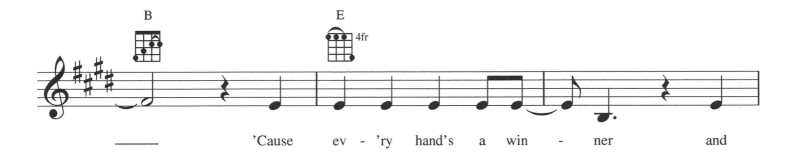

___ 'Cause ev - 'ry hand's a win - ner and

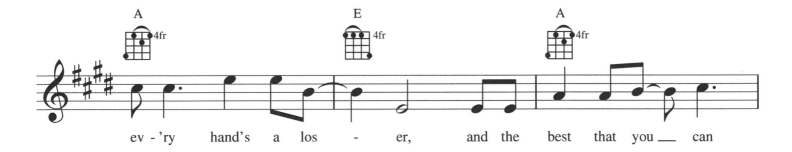

ev - 'ry hand's a los - er, and the best that you ___ can

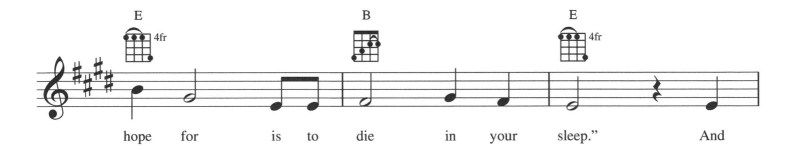

hope for is to die in your sleep." And

when he'd fin - ished speak - in', he turned back towards the win -

- dow, crushed out his cig - a - rette, and

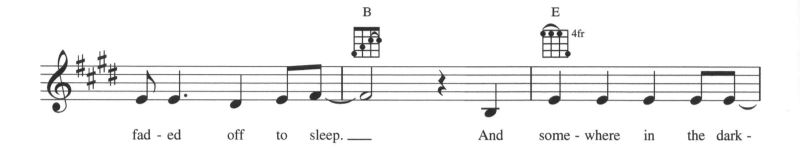

fad - ed off to sleep. And some - where in the dark -

- ness, the gam - bler, he broke e - ven. But

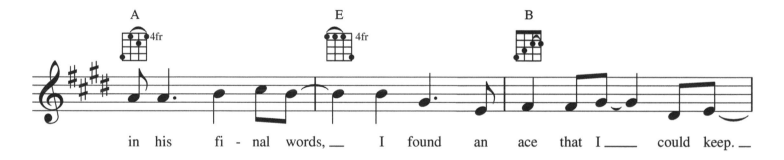

in his fi - nal words, I found an ace that I could keep.

Chorus

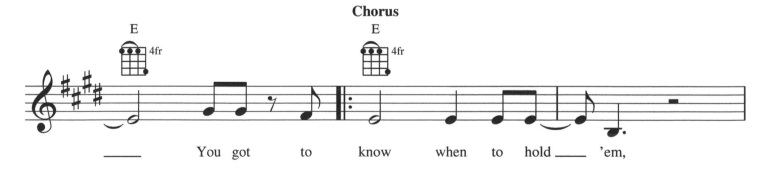

You got to know when to hold 'em,

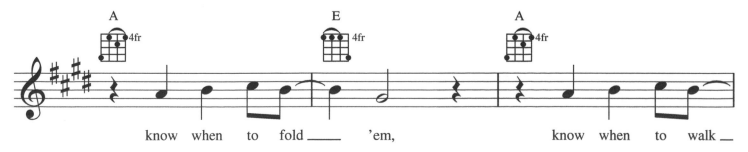

know when to fold 'em, know when to walk

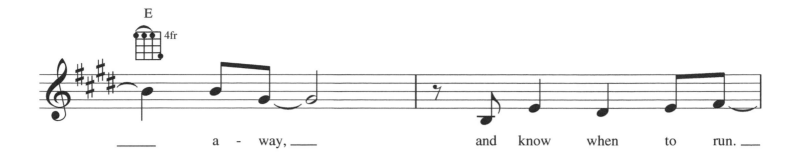

_____ a - way, _____ and know when to run. _____

_____ You nev - er count your

mon - ey when you're sit - tin' at the ta -

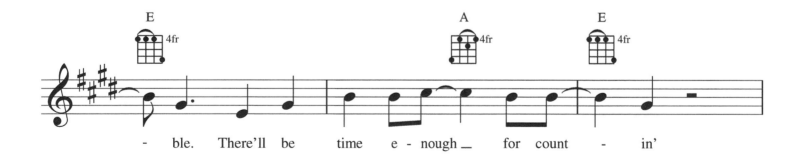

- ble. There'll be time e - nough _____ for count - in'

when the deal - in's done. You got to done.

Funny How Time Slips Away

Words and Music by Willie Nelson

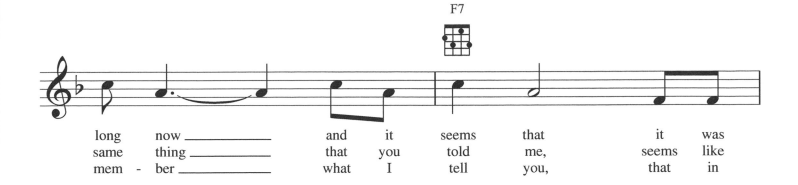

long   now _____   and   it   seems   that   it   was
same   thing _____   that   you   seems   told   me,   seems   like
mem - ber _____   what   I   tell   you,   that   in

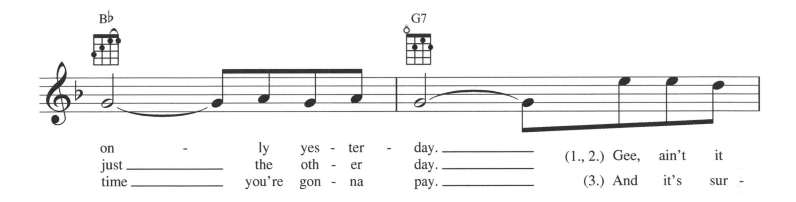

on - ly   yes - ter - day. _____   (1., 2.) Gee,   ain't   it
just _____   the   oth - er   day. _____   (3.) And   it's   sur -
time _____   you're   gon - na   pay. _____

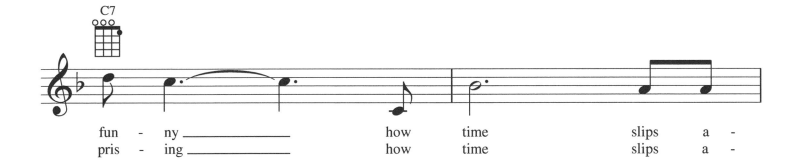

fun - ny _____   how   time   slips   a -
pris - ing _____   how   time   slips   a -

way? _____   2. How's   your _____
way. _____   3. Got - ta

Green Green Grass of Home

Words and Music by Curly Putman

First note

Verse
Moderately slow ♩ = 86

1. The old home - town looks the same as I step down from the
(2.) old house is still stand - ing though the paint is cracked and
3. *See additional lyrics*

train, and there to meet me was my ma - ma and
dry, and there's that old oak tree that I used to

pa - pa. Down the road I look and
play on. Down the road lane I walk with

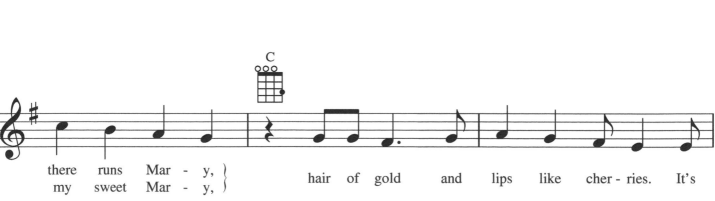

there runs Mar - y, }
my sweet Mar - y, } hair of gold and lips like cher - ries. It's

good to touch the green, green grass of home.

Chorus

Yes, they'll all come to

(1., 2.) meet me, arms a
(3.) see me in the

reach - ing, smil - ing sweet - ly. It's good to touch the
shade of that old oak tree as they lay me 'neath the

1., 2.

green, green grass of home.

2. The
3. Then I a -

3.

home.

Additional Lyrics

3. Spoken: *Then I awake, and look around me at the grey walls that surround me,*
    And I realize that I was only dreaming.
    For there's a guard and there's a sad, old padre. Arm in arm we'll walk at daybreak.
    Again I'll touch the green, green grass of home.

Heartaches by the Number

Words and Music by Harlan Howard

Hey, Good Lookin'

Words and Music by Hank Williams

Bridge

1. I got a hot rod Ford and a two dol - lar bill, and
2. I'm gon - na throw my date book _ o - ver the fence and

I know a spot right o - ver the hill. _ There's so - da pop and the
find me _ one for five or ten cents. _ I'll keep it 'til it's _

danc - in's free, _ so if you wan - na have fun, come a - long with me. _
cov - ered with age, _ 'cause I'm writ - in' your name down on ev - 'ry page. _

Verse

2., 4. Hey, good look - in' what - cha got

cook - in'? How's a - bout cook - in' some - thin' up _ with

1.

me? _

3. I'm

2.

me? _

(Hey, Won't You Play)
Another Somebody Done Somebody Wrong Song

Words and Music by Larry Butler and Chips Moman

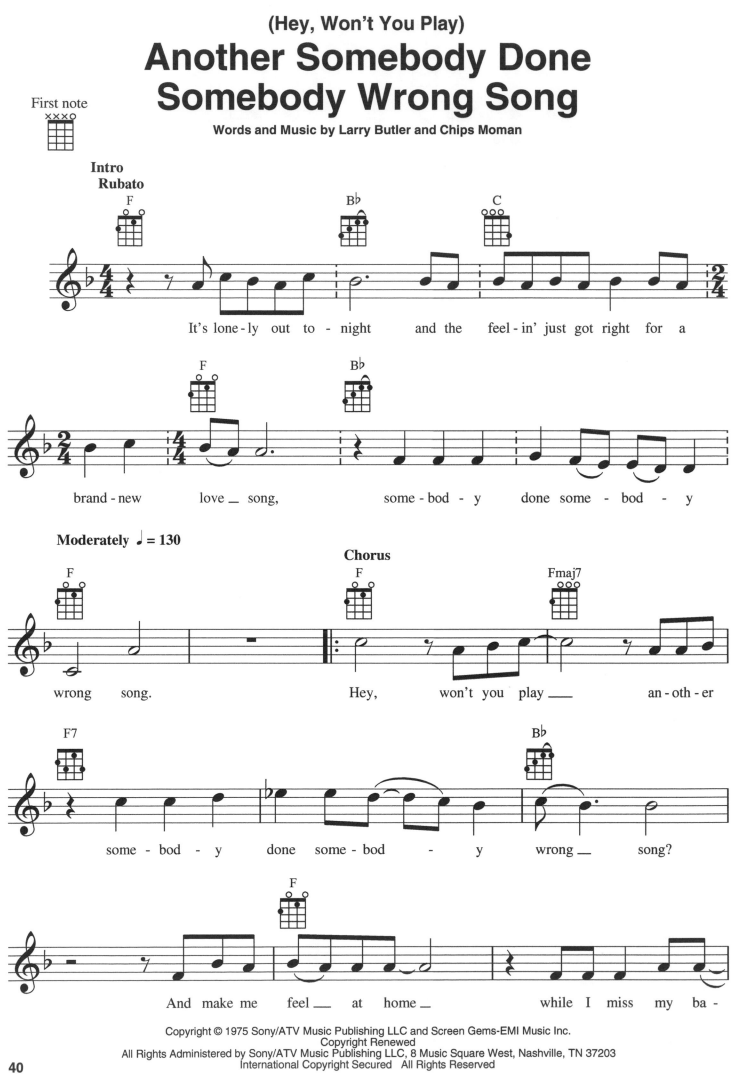

- by while I miss my ba - by.

Verse

1., 2. So, play, ____ play for me ____ a sad ____ mel - o - dy, ____

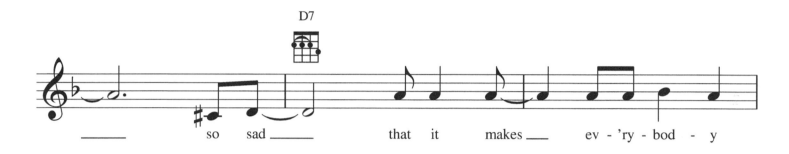

____ so sad ____ that it makes ____ ev - 'ry - bod - y

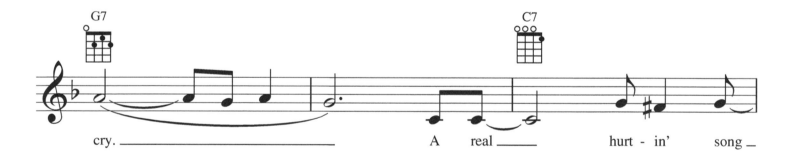

cry. ____ A real ____ hurt - in' song ____

____ a - bout a love that's gone ____ wrong, ____ 'cause

I don't ____ want ____ to cry ____ all a - lone. ____

Chorus

F   Fmaj7

1. Hey,   won't you play _____   an - oth - er
2., 3. -   by.

F7

some - bod - y   done   some - bod - y

Bb

wrong _____ song?   And make me

F

feel _____ at home _____   while I miss my ba -

Gm   C7   *Play 3 times*   F

-    by,   while I miss my ba - by.

I Walk the Line

Words and Music by John R. Cash

First note

Verse
Moderately fast ♩ = 104

1. I keep a close watch on this heart of mine. _____

_____ I keep my eyes wide o - pen all _____ the

time. _____ I keep the ends out

for the tie _____ that binds. _____ Be - cause _____ you're

mine, _____ I walk the line.

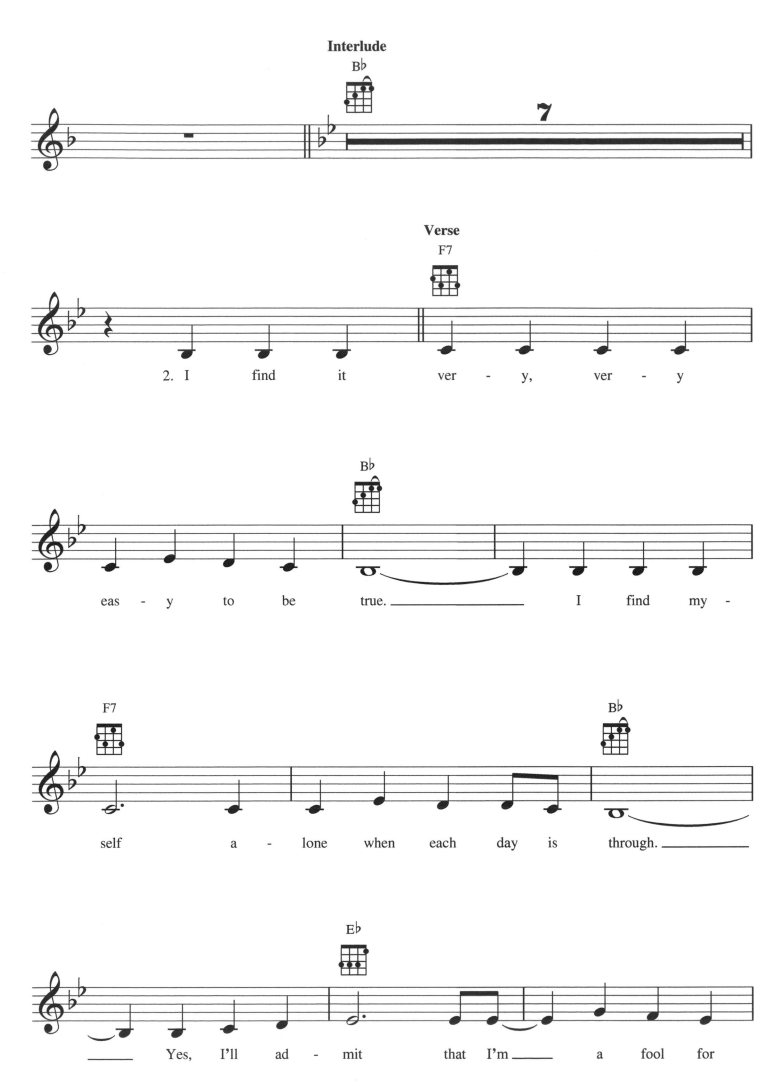

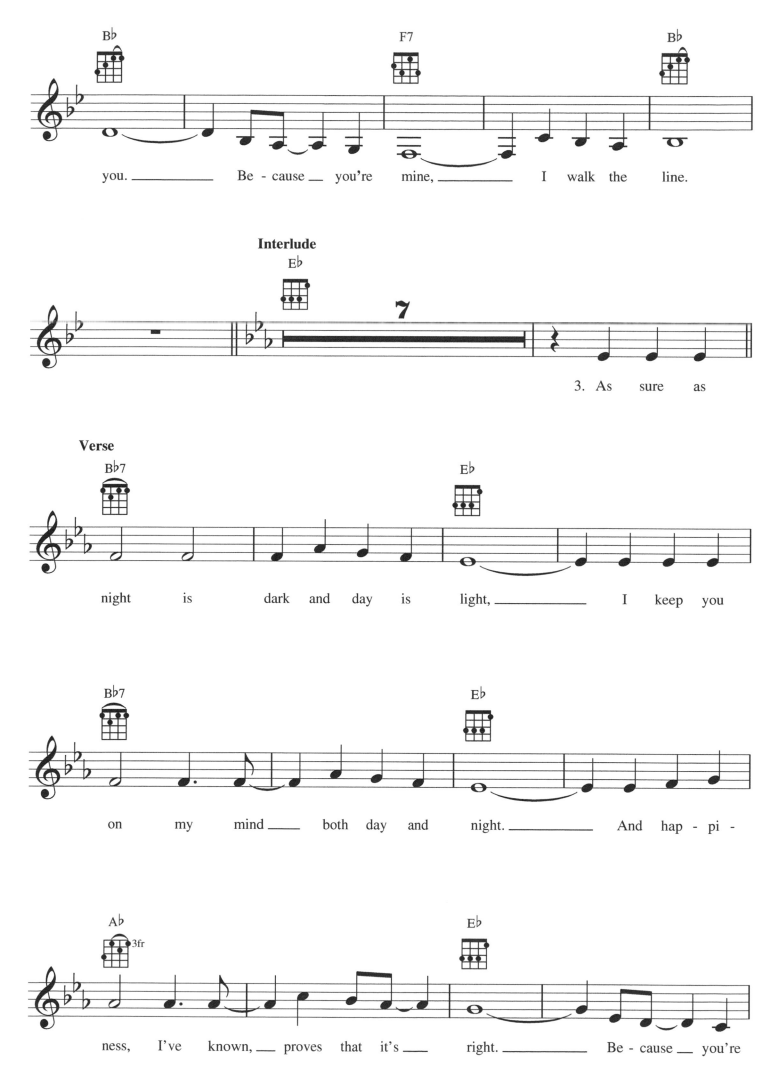

you. _____ Be - cause __ you're mine, _____ I walk the line.

Interlude

7

3. As sure as

Verse

night is dark and day is light, _____ I keep you

on my mind ____ both day and night. _____ And hap - pi -

ness, I've known, __ proves that it's __ right. _____ Be - cause __ you're

Interlude

mine, _____ I walk the line.

Verse

4. You've got a way to keep ___ me on your side. _____

_____ You give me cause for love that I can't hide. _____

_____ For you, I know, I'd e - ven try ___ to turn the tide. _____

_____ Be - cause ___ you're mine, _____ I walk the line.

I Can't Help It
(If I'm Still in Love with You)

Words and Music by Hank Williams

Bridge

1. A pic - ture from the past came slow - ly
(2.) hard to know an - oth - er's lips will

steal - ing _____ as I brushed your arm and
kiss you _____ and ____ hold you just and the

walked so close to you. _____ Then
way I used to do. _____ Oh,

sud - den - ly ____ I got that old - time feel - ing. ____
heav - en on - ly knows how much I miss you. ____

____ } I can't help it if I'm still in love with you. __

1.
2.

_____ 2. It's ____

It Wasn't God Who Made Honky Tonk Angels

Words and Music by J.D. Miller

it brings mem - 'ries when I was a trust - ing
was be - cause there al - ways was a man to

wife. _____
blame. _____ It was - n't God who made hon - ky tonk

an - gels _____ as you wrote in the words of your

song. _____ Too man - y times mar - ried men think they're still

sin - gle. _____ That has caused man - y a good girl to go

wrong. _____ 2. It's a wrong. _____

Jambalaya
(On the Bayou)

Words and Music by Hank Williams

First note

King of the Road

Words and Music by Roger Miller

two hours ___ of push-ing broom ___ buys a 8 _____ by 12 _____
old sto - gies I have found, ___ short ___ but not too

four - bit room. ___ ⎫
big a - round. ___ ⎬ I'm a man of means ___ by no means,

1.

2.

king of the road. ____ ____ 3. I know

Verse

ev - er - y en - gi - neer on ev - er - y train, ___ all of the chil - dren and

all of their names, and ev - er - y hand - out in ev - er - y town and

ev - 'ry lock that ain't locked when no one's a - round. ___ 4. I sing

Verse

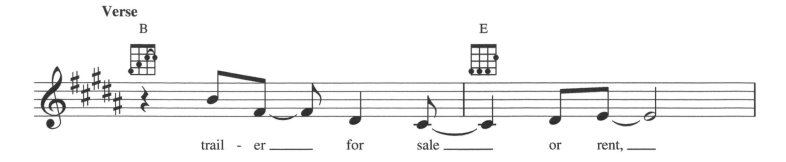

trail - er _____ for sale _____ or rent, _____

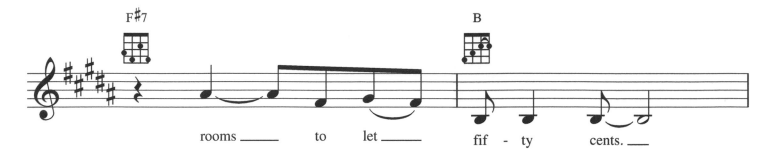

rooms _____ to let _____ fif - ty cents. _____

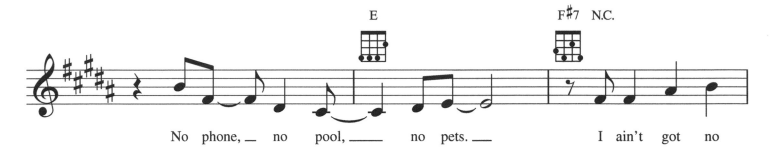

No phone, _ no pool, _____ no pets. _ I ain't got no

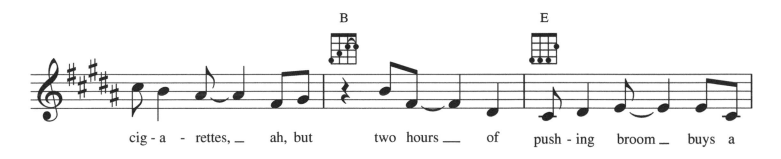

cig - a - rettes, _ ah, but two hours _ of push - ing broom _ buys a

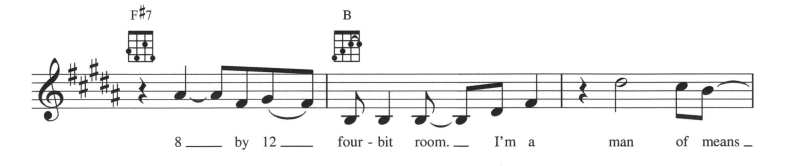

8 _____ by 12 _____ four - bit room. _ I'm a man of means _

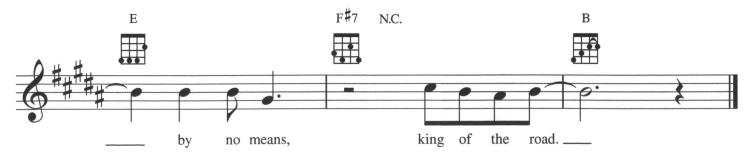

_____ by no means, king of the road. _____

Mammas Don't Let Your
Babies Grow Up to Be Cowboys

Words and Music by Ed Bruce and Patsy Bruce

First note

Verse
Moderately fast ♩. = 60

D

1. Cow - boys ain't eas - y to love and they're

G

hard - er _____ to hold.

A7

They'd rath - er _____ give you a song than dia - monds and

D

gold.

Lone Star belt buck - les, and old fad - ed Le - vi's, _____ and

each night be - gins a new day.   If you

don't un - der - stand him, ___ and he don't die ___ young, he'll

prob - a - bly just ride ___ a - way.

Chorus

Ma - mas, ___ don't let your

ba - bies grow up to be ___ cow - boys.

Don't let 'em pick gui - tars and

drive them old trucks. Let 'em be doc - tors, and

law - yers, and such. Ma - mas, _____

don't let your ba - bies grow up to be ____ cow - boys.

'Cause they'll nev - er stay

home, and they're al - ways a - lone, e - ven with

some - one they love. _____

Verse

2. Cow - boys like smok - y old pool - rooms __ and clear moun - tain __

morn - ings.

Lit - tle warm pup - pies, and chil - dren, and __ girls of the night. __

Them that don't

know him won't like him and them that do some - times won't

know how ___ to take him. He ain't wrong, he's just

diff - 'rent, but his ___ pride won't let him do things to make

you think he's right.

Chorus

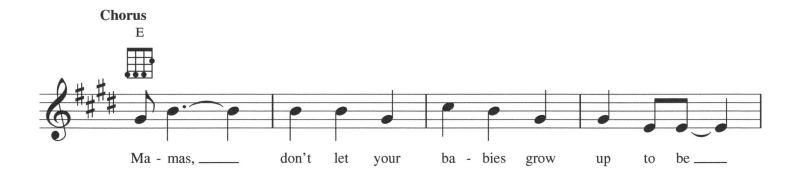

Ma - mas, ___ don't let your ba - bies grow up to be ___

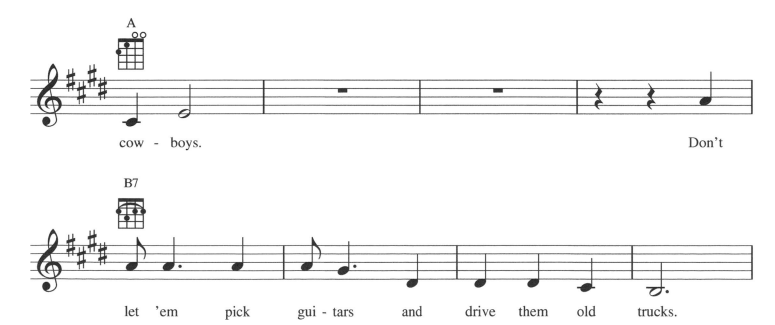

cow - boys. Don't

let 'em pick gui - tars and drive them old trucks.

Let 'em   be   doc - tors,   and   law - yers,   and   such.

Ma - mas, _____   don't   let   your   ba - bies   grow

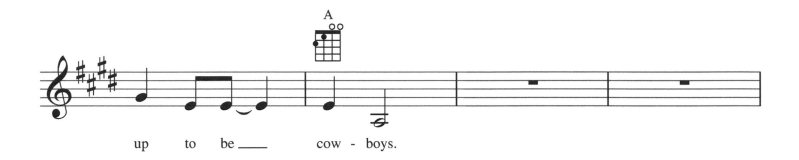

up   to   be _____   cow - boys.

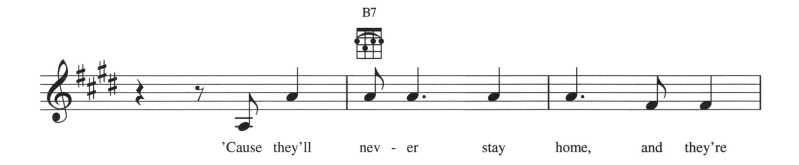

'Cause they'll   nev - er   stay   home,   and   they're

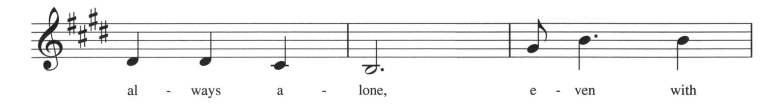

al - ways   a - lone,   e - ven   with

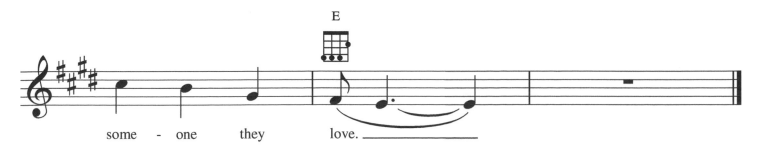

some - one   they   love. _____

Oh, Lonesome Me

Words and Music by Don Gibson

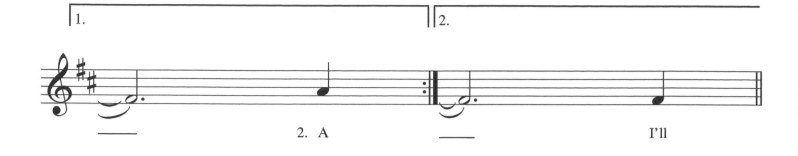

1.

2.

2. A   I'll

Bridge

A   E7

bet she's not like me, she's out and fan - cy

free, flirt - ing with the boys with all her

A

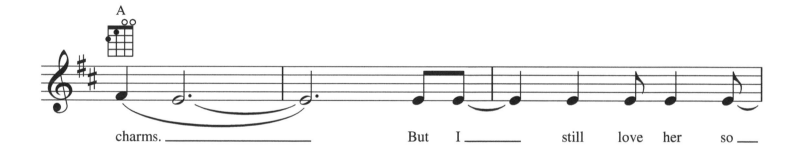

charms.   But I still love her so

E7

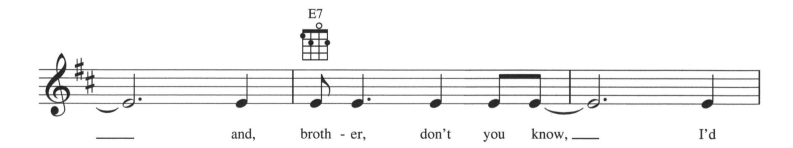

and, broth - er, don't you know, I'd

A

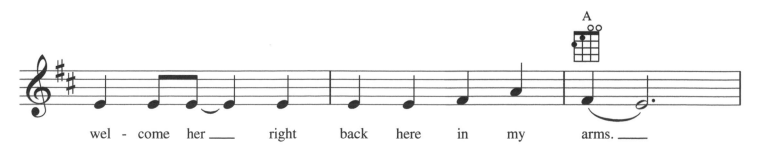

wel - come her right back here in my arms.

Make the World Go Away

Words and Music by Hank Cochran

Release Me

Words and Music by Robert Yount, Eddie Miller and Dub Williams

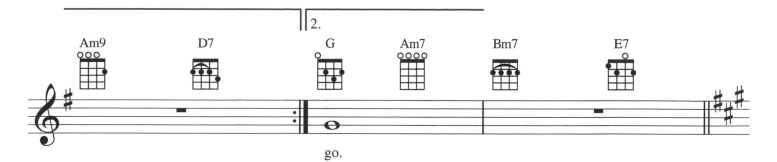

go.

Verse

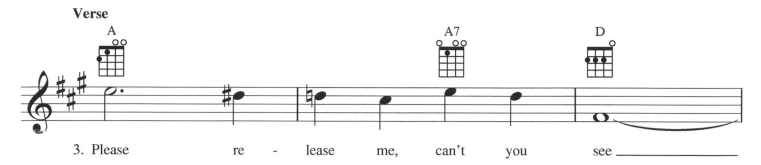

3. Please re - lease me, can't you see _____

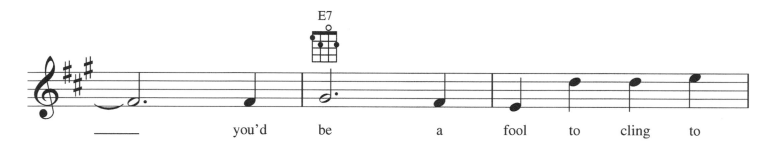

_____ you'd be a fool to cling to

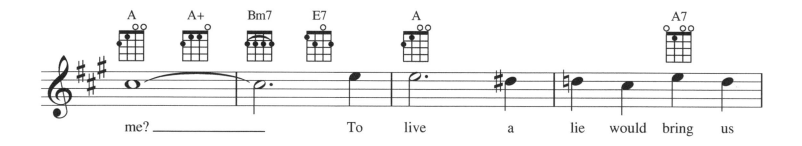

me? _____ To live a lie would bring us

pain. _____ Re - lease me and let me love a -

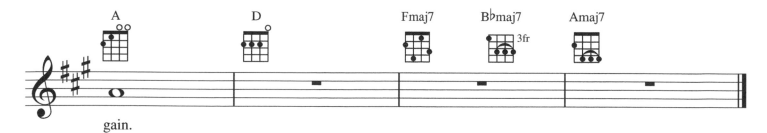

gain.

Rocky Top

Words and Music by Boudleaux Bryant and Felice Bryant

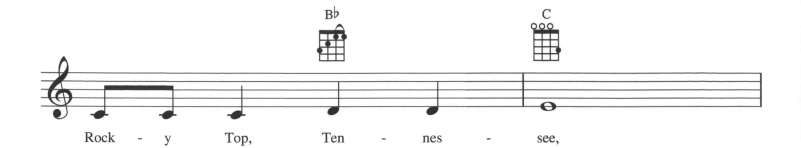

Rock - y Top, Ten - nes - see,

To Coda ⊕ | 1. | 2. | *D.S. al Coda*

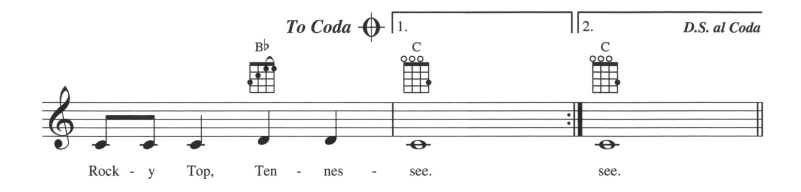

Rock - y Top, Ten - nes - see. | see.

⊕ **Coda**

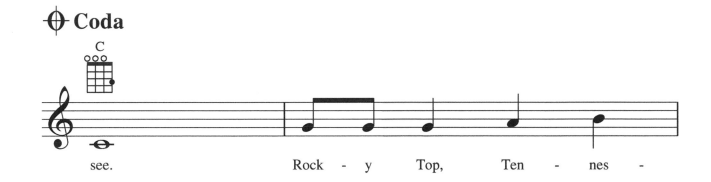

see. | Rock - y Top, Ten - nes -

see. _____

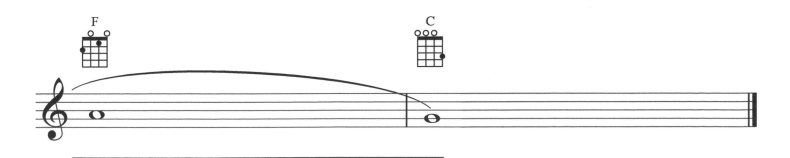

Smoky Mountain Rain

Words and Music by Kye Fleming and Dennis Morgan

First note

1. I thumbed my way from L. A. back to Knox-ville. I found out those bright lights ain't where ___ I be-long. ___ From a phone booth in the rain, ___ I called to tell her.

2. I waved a die-sel down out-side a ca-fe. He said that he was go-ing as far as ___ Gat-lin-burg. ___ I climbed up in the cab all wet, and cold, and lone-ly.

I've had a change of dreams. __ I'm com - ing home, __
I wiped my eyes and told ____ him a - bout her. __

____ but tears filled my eyes ____ when I
____ "I've got to find her. Can you make

found out she was gone. _____
these big wheels burn?" _____

Chorus

Smok - y Moun - tain rain ____ keeps on fall - ing,

I keep on call - ing _____ her

name. _____ Smok - y Moun - tain rain, __

I'll   keep   on   search - ing,

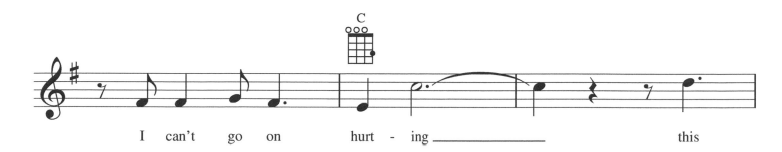

I   can't   go   on   hurt - ing _____ this

way. _____ She's   some - where   in   the

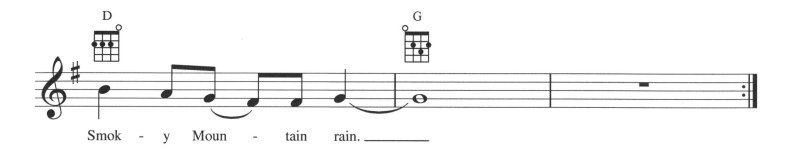

Smok - y   Moun - tain   rain. _____

Bridge

I   can't   blame   her   for   let - ting   go.

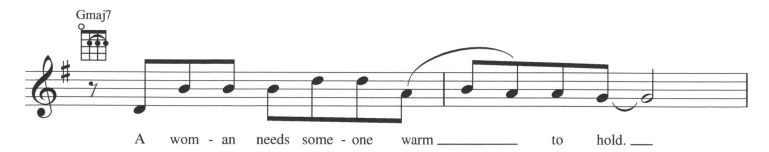

A   wom - an   needs   some - one   warm _____ to   hold. ___

I feel the rain run - ning down ___ my face. ___

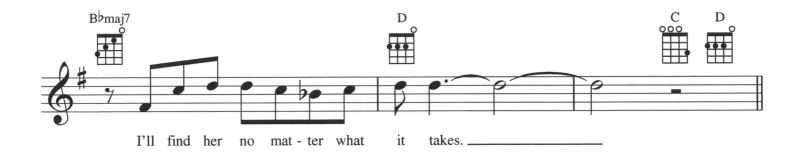

I'll find her no mat - ter what it takes. ___

Chorus

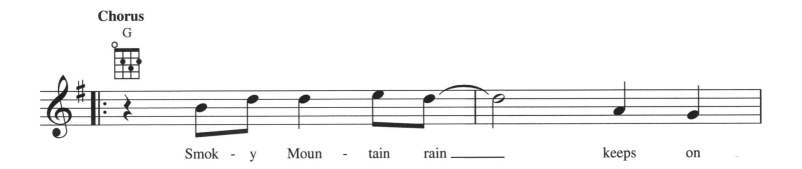

Smok - y Moun - tain rain ___ keeps on

fall - ing, I keep on call - ing ___

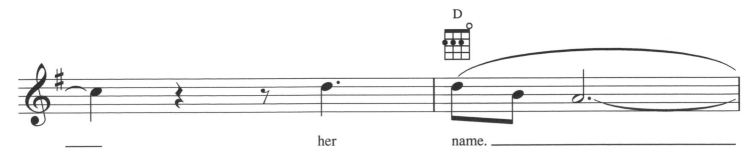

___ her name. ___

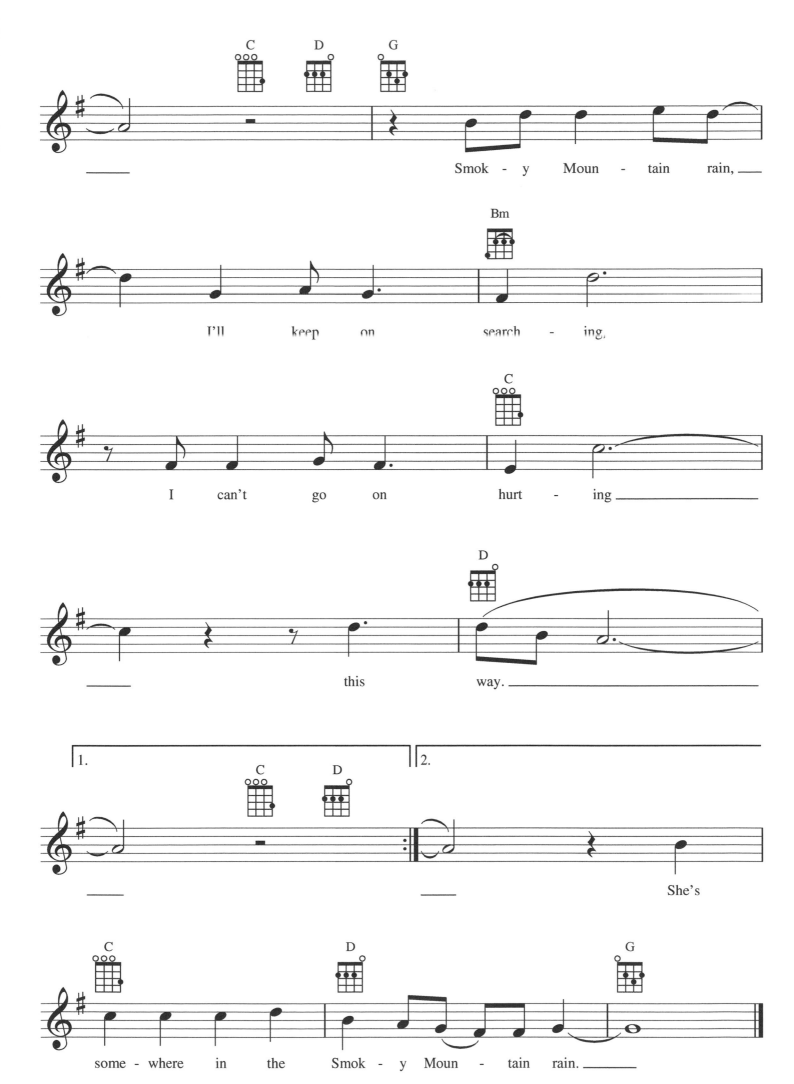

Smok - y Moun - tain rain, ___

I'll keep on search - ing,

I can't go on hurt - ing ___

___ this way. ___

1. 2. She's

some - where in the Smok - y Moun - tain rain. ___

Tennessee Waltz

Words and Music by Redd Stewart and Pee Wee King

First note

Verse
Slow Waltz ♩ = 120

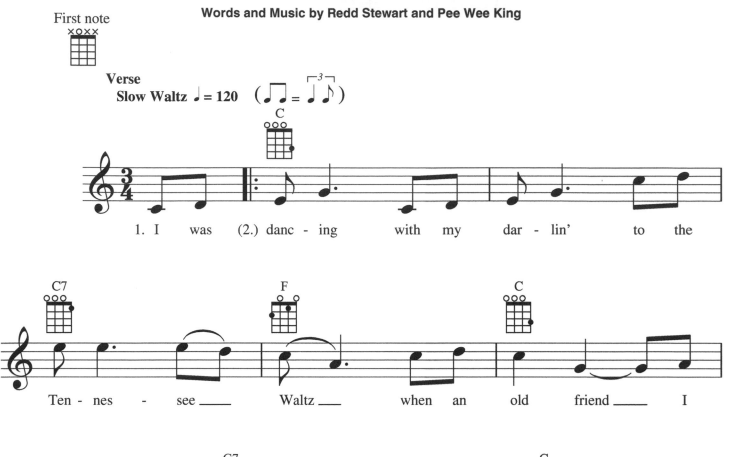

1. I was (2.) danc - ing with my dar - lin' to the

Ten - nes - see ___ Waltz ___ when an old friend ___ I

hap - pened to see. ___ I in - tro - duced him to my

loved one ___ and while they were ___ danc - ing, ___ my

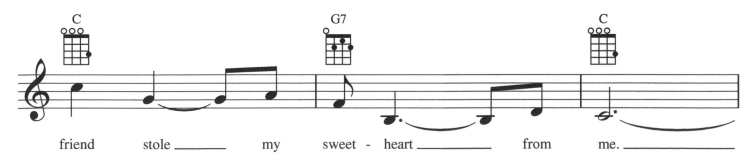

friend stole ___ my sweet - heart ___ from me. ___

Chorus

I re - mem - ber _____ the night and the

Ten - nes - see Waltz. On - ly you know _____ how

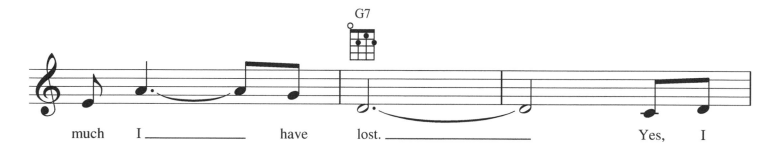

much I _____ have lost. _____ Yes, I

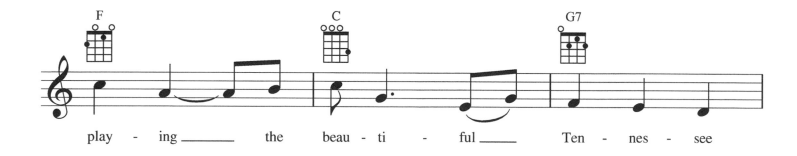

lost my lit - tle dar - lin' _____ the night they were ____

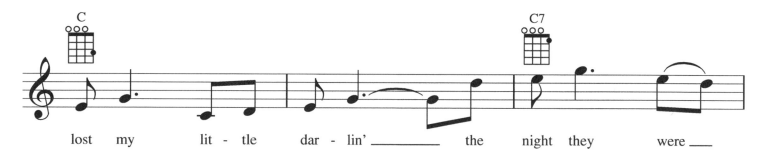

play - ing ____ the beau - ti - ful ____ Ten - nes - see

Waltz. _____ 2. I was ____

79

Welcome to My World

Words and Music by Ray Winkler and John Hathcock

Wel - come to my world, _____ won't you come on
in? _____ Mir - a - cles, I guess, _____
_____ still hap - pen now and then. _____ Step in - to my
heart. _____ Leave your cares be - hind. _____
_____ Wel - come to my world _____ built with you in

Bridge

mind. _____ Knock and the door __ will o - pen, _____

seek and you will find. Ask and you'll be

giv - en _____ the key to this world of mine. _____

Chorus

_____ I'll be wait - ing here _____ with my arms un -

furled, _____ wait - ing just for you. _____ Wel - come to my

1.

world. _____ Wel - come to my

2.

world. _____

81

You Are My Sunshine

Words and Music by Jimmie Davis

Your Cheatin' Heart

Words and Music by Hank Williams

Walkin' After Midnight

Lyrics by Don Hecht
Music by Alan W. Block

First note

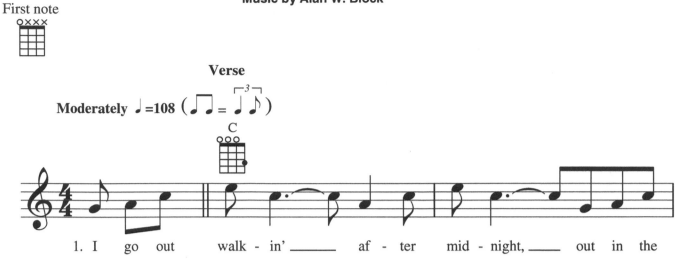

Verse

Moderately ♩=108

1. I go out walk-in' _____ af-ter mid-night, _____ out in the

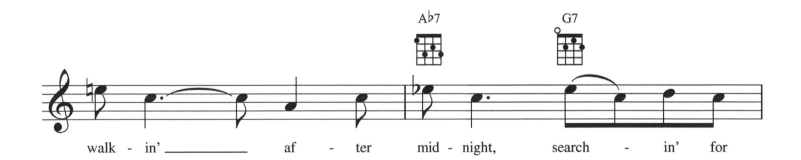

moon-light, _____ just _____ like we used to do. I'm al-ways

walk-in' _____ af-ter mid-night, search-in' for

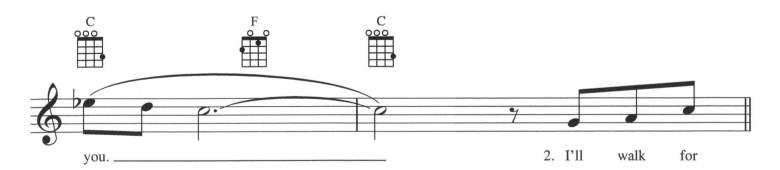

you. _____ 2. I'll walk for

as the skies turn gloom - y, night winds whis - per to me. I'm

1.

lone - some _____ as _____ I _____ can be. _____ 3. I go out

2.

_____ 4. I go out walk - in' _____ af - ter

mid - night, _____ out in the moon - light, _____ just _____

hop - in' you may be some - where a walk - in' _____ af - ter

Outro-Verse

mid - night search - in' ___ for ___ me. _____